Building a Brand in the Metaverse

How Creators, Coaches, and Businesses Can Thrive in the New Digital Economy

By Joe Correa

Published by Live Stronger Faster

This book is for educational and informational purposes only. The author and publisher are not engaged in rendering legal, financial, or other professional advice. Readers should consult a qualified professional before making any financial decisions.

First Edition

Table of Contents

Introduction...5

Chapter 1: The New Rules of Branding in the Metaverse................10

Chapter 2: Crafting Your Metaverse Identity: Avatars, Aesthetics & Brand Essence...20

Chapter 3: Building Your Metaverse Headquarters: Worlds, Spaces, and Interactive Brand Environments..29

Chapter 4: Designing Metaverse Experiences: Events, Workshops, Gatherings, and Immersive Encounters..38

Chapter 5: Building Community in the Metaverse: Culture, Connection & Long-Term Engagement..47

Chapter 6: Monetizing Your Metaverse Brand: Products, Services, NFTs, Memberships & Digital Assets..56

Chapter 7: Scaling Your Metaverse Brand: Automation, AI Integration, Partnerships & World Expansion...............................65

Chapter 8: Marketing Your Metaverse Brand: Visibility, Social Reach, Storytelling & World Discovery..74

Chapter 9: Protecting Your Metaverse Brand: Security, Ethics, Boundaries & Community Safety..83

Chapter 10: The Future of Metaverse Branding: Longevity, Legacy & Multi-World Evolution...91

Epilogue..100

Introduction

The metaverse is no longer a distant fantasy or a buzzword reserved for tech insiders. It is rapidly becoming the next major frontier of identity, commerce, entertainment, education, and community building. For creators, entrepreneurs, coaches, consultants, and everyday individuals looking to build something meaningful, the metaverse represents the most powerful opportunity since the invention of social media — and in many ways, it is even bigger. Because unlike the traditional internet where your brand exists on borrowed land, dictated by algorithms and controlled by major platforms, the metaverse allows you to build an identity, a business, and a community that you truly own. Book 7 of this series is about mastering this new digital landscape, understanding how brand-building evolves in immersive environments, and learning the tools and strategies you need to create a magnetic presence in the virtual world. Whether you want to build influence, attract clients, sell products, host events, or create your own digital universe, the metaverse opens doors that were impossible just a few years ago.

Today's most successful brands are no longer built through logos, color palettes, and perfectly curated social media feeds alone. In Web3, your brand is an *experience* — a living, evolving ecosystem of interactions, environments, stories, and community participation. When someone steps into your virtual studio, your digital headquarters, your branded world, or your immersive learning space, they don't just see your brand — they *feel* it. They move through it. They experience it with all senses. Your audience becomes an active participant in your universe, not a passive follower. And in this deeper level of interaction, trust grows faster, loyalty strengthens, and monetization opportunities multiply. This shift gives creators, coaches, and businesses unprecedented leverage. It means you can build a brand that is not just consumed but *inhabited.* A brand that your audience wants to return to daily. A brand they want to share, engage with, and be part of. This is the essence of metaverse branding: a shift from audiences watching you to audiences *joining you.*

But building a brand in the metaverse is not simply about learning technology. It is about understanding humanity — why people gather, what makes them feel connected, and how identity changes when it becomes digital. For the first time in history, people are creating avatars that reflect who they are, who they wish to become, or aspects of themselves they have never expressed before. This new form of self-expression creates opportunities for brands to connect with people on deeper emotional and psychological levels. Your metaverse brand is not just about what you sell — it is about the world you build, the values you express, and the identity you empower your community to embody. Whether your audience is stepping into your virtual fitness studio, joining your live coaching session in a digital amphitheater, attending your art gallery opening, trying your virtual products, or interacting with AI versions of your team, every moment becomes a brand touchpoint. Every interaction becomes part of your story. And every experience becomes a reason for your community to stay.

Creators and entrepreneurs who understand this early will have an enormous advantage. In the same way that early YouTubers dominated their niche, early Amazon sellers captured entire industries, and early Instagram influencers became household names, early metaverse brand builders will shape the next generation of digital influence. The metaverse is not overcrowded. It's not saturated. It's barely begun. There are entire categories that do not yet exist, entire audiences waiting to be served, and entire industries ready to be reinvented. Whether you're a coach wanting to host immersive workshops, a fitness instructor building a virtual training universe, a consultant offering holographic office hours, a musician creating interactive concerts, a speaker presenting in virtual auditoriums, a real estate agent showcasing digital and physical listings, or a business owner building a community hub where customers can gather, learn, and buy — the metaverse is a canvas with infinite potential. What you build now can grow exponentially for years to come.

Building a brand in the metaverse also introduces new tools and strategies that did not exist in Web2. Instead of traditional websites, you have virtual headquarters. Instead of flat images and profile pictures, you have avatars, skins, emotes, and 3D identities. Instead of newsletters, you have immersive communities where people engage in real time. Instead of simple digital products, you have NFTs, access passes, token-gated memberships, virtual merchandise, and interactive content that rewards participation. Instead of followers, you have *citizens* of your world — people who learn, socialize, create, collaborate, and even co-own aspects of your metaverse brand through decentralized models. These new tools allow you to build deeper loyalty, more sustainable income streams, and stronger communities than anything the traditional creator economy offered. In this book, you will learn exactly how those tools work and how you can use them to build a powerful, profitable, future-proof brand.

One of the most important elements of brand-building in the metaverse is storytelling — not in a marketing sense, but in a world-building sense. Your metaverse brand is a story your audience steps inside. It is the feeling your world gives them the moment they enter. It is the music, the architecture, the lighting, the textures, the interactivity, and the sense of belonging you create. It is the vision you share about the future. And it is the role your community plays in that future. When someone enters your world, do they feel like they've stepped into your digital identity? Can they recognize your values and your voice without reading a word of text? Does your world invite exploration, curiosity, and participation? These are the questions that separate forgettable brands from iconic ones. Inside the metaverse, you have the ability to create environments that extend your story, amplify your mission, and immerse your audience in a narrative they want to be part of.

Finally, building a brand in the metaverse is about independence and opportunity. For the first time ever, creators and entrepreneurs can build businesses that are platform-resistant, global, scalable, and not limited by physical constraints. You can reach thousands of people around the world instantly. You can sell assets that require no shipping, no inventory, and no fulfillment. You can build communities that operate 24/7. You can automate parts of your brand with AI assistants, virtual staff, and interactive experiences. You can host events, build products, offer coaching, and run entire businesses inside virtual worlds. And you can do all of this while maintaining control, ownership, and creative freedom over your digital empire. That is the promise of metaverse branding — and in this book, you will learn how to turn that promise into your reality.

Chapter 1

The New Rules of Branding in the Metaverse

Branding in the metaverse requires a complete shift in the way creators, coaches, entrepreneurs, and businesses think about identity, community, and value. In the traditional digital world, branding revolved around visuals, messaging, and consistency: your logo, typography, color palette, social media presence, website design, and advertising style. But in the metaverse, a brand is no longer just something your audience sees — it is something they experience. It's not a static identity but a living environment. People don't merely scroll through your brand; they step inside it, move around it, interact with it, and build memories in it. This shift requires a deeper understanding of immersion, world-building, psychology, and community-driven engagement. The old rules still matter, but they are no longer enough. The metaverse introduces new rules where experience outranks aesthetics, presence outranks content, and interaction outranks broadcasting.

The first key rule of metaverse branding is that your brand becomes a *space*, not just a message. Your brand is represented through the worlds you build, the experiences you create, and the ways people can interact with your digital universe. Instead of websites, metaverse brands have virtual headquarters, community hubs, social plazas, immersive classrooms, training centers, digital stores, and entertainment arenas. The architecture itself becomes part of your branding, whether futuristic, minimalist, nature-inspired, professional, fantasy-themed, or gamified. Even small details — like lighting, soundscapes, textures, avatar animations, and pathways — shape how people perceive and emotionally connect with your presence. Your audience doesn't just observe your brand; they inhabit it. They socialize inside it. They attend events, take classes, shop for products, and engage with your community through an entire world crafted by you.

The second rule is that your brand identity is represented through your avatar — or avatars — in ways that often feel more personal than physical branding. In Web2, you were limited to profile pictures and short bios. In Web3, your avatar communicates values, energy, personality, and authority instantly. Your avatar can be realistic, stylized, futuristic, animated, or symbolic — whatever best represents your desired brand essence. For some creators, choosing an avatar that resembles their real self builds trust. For others, choosing a unique digital persona creates curiosity, differentiation, and creative freedom. Because people interact with your avatar in real time, your digital self becomes a primary branding asset.

It controls how people remember you, how they perceive your confidence, how they interpret your teaching style, and how they feel when they encounter your presence in the metaverse. In many cases, your avatar becomes your global identity, instantly recognizable across multiple platforms.

The third rule of metaverse branding is that community becomes the core of your brand value. In traditional branding, businesses communicated *to* their audiences. In the metaverse, businesses communicate *with* their communities. People gather inside your world, talk to each other, share experiences, participate in events, and co-create aspects of your brand. This participation creates stronger loyalty than any Web2 system ever provided. Community members become contributors, ambassadors, volunteers, moderators, creators, and evangelists. They feel ownership in your world because they spend time inside it, helping it grow. This creates a self-sustaining ecosystem where engagement fuels more engagement. The more your community interacts inside your world, the more your brand becomes woven into their digital lives. Metaverse brands that cultivate strong communities outperform those that simply broadcast content from a distance.

The fourth rule is the rise of interactive and experiential products. In Web2, creators sold ebooks, courses, webinars, merchandise, consulting sessions, and physical products. In the metaverse, these offerings evolve into immersive equivalents: interactive courses taught inside virtual studios, coaching sessions held inside 3D amphitheaters, digital merchandise for avatars, NFT-based loyalty passes, gamified learning modules, virtual stockrooms for product demos, and token-gated communities that reward participation. These experiences transform passive consumption into active involvement. Instead of watching a video, your audience participates in a virtual lesson. Instead of reading a guide, they walk through an interactive environment. Instead of owning merchandise, they wear digital assets on their avatar. The more immersive the product, the stronger the brand connection.

The fifth rule is that trust is built through transparency and presence. In the metaverse, brands cannot hide behind polished content alone. People interact with you in real time, speak with you face-to-face in virtual form, and observe your behavior inside digital environments. They see your world, your values, your decisions, and your authenticity. This transparency builds trust faster because it feels personal and human. People feel like they truly know you. And because the metaverse operates through decentralization, smart contracts, and community governance, ethical brands gain a powerful advantage. Transparency becomes part of your brand equity —

and your actions inside your world carry more weight than your messaging. The sixth rule is that metaverse branding is deeply influenced by emotional design. People connect with virtual worlds through feelings — curiosity, excitement, safety, belonging, exploration, nostalgia, ambition, and identity expression. Your world must evoke emotions that align with your mission. A wellness brand may use nature-inspired visual themes, calming soundscapes, soft textures, and guided meditation experiences. A business coaching brand may build futuristic arenas, high-energy environments, holographic displays, and achievement-driven mechanics that reinforce growth and success. A fitness brand may build adrenaline-fueled arenas, obstacle courses, strength-training simulations, and motivational group sessions. Emotional design influences how long people stay, how often they return, and how deeply they trust your brand.

The seventh rule is cross-platform identity. Your metaverse brand must exist across multiple platforms — Decentraland, VRChat, Spatial, Meta Horizon, The Sandbox, and whatever new worlds emerge. Your branding must be recognizable regardless of the environment. This requires consistent design principles, avatar style, storytelling tone, values, and community interaction patterns. When someone encounters your brand in any world, they should know it's you instantly. This requires planning, strategy, and a clear understanding of how your brand translates into 3D environments. The final rule is that your brand becomes part of a long-term digital legacy. Everything you build — your worlds, NFTs, avatars, experiences, content, systems, communities, and partnerships — becomes part of your digital estate. Your metaverse brand is not fragile like a social media account. It is not dependent on one platform's algorithm. It is distributed, decentralized, multi-platform, and capable of growing for decades. Your brand becomes a digital empire, one that you control, one that grows with the evolution of virtual worlds, and one that gives you long-term ownership, influence, and income. Mastering these new rules gives you a powerful advantage as the metaverse moves into mainstream adoption.

"The World of Aurelia"

Aurelia was nothing like the worlds she visited before. It was breathtaking — an endless horizon of floating gardens, shimmering walkways, glowing waterfalls, and crystalline towers that reflected colors she had never seen on Earth. As Maya stepped through the portal, her avatar's footsteps echoed softly along a luminous path. She glanced around in awe, taking in the architecture, the music, the ambient energy in the air. Everything around her felt like a living dream. She was here to meet the creator of this world — someone whose metaverse brand had become legendary — and she wanted to understand how such a place could be built from imagination alone. She had spent years building her personal brand on social media, posting videos, sharing ideas, trying to stand out. But none of it compared to what she felt now. Aurelia wasn't content; it was an experience. It was the future of branding — and she knew it the moment she arrived.

A gentle voice called out from behind a towering crystal tree. "Welcome to Aurelia, Maya." She turned to see an avatar walking toward her, its design elegant yet simple — a humanoid figure with glowing golden outlines, eyes like warm lantern light, and movements that flowed like water. It was both surreal and calming. This was Solara, the creator of Aurelia, a coach whose metaverse brand had drawn thousands into her world. Maya instinctively knew she was in the presence of someone who had mastered something she was only beginning to understand. Solara motioned for her to walk with her, and they moved together through the floating gardens, passing groups of visitors meditating, studying, collaborating, and exploring. "This world is my brand," Solara said softly. "Not the billboards, not the logos, not the marketing. This. The experiences. The feelings it creates. The community that gathers here. A brand is not what you tell people — it's what they feel when they step into your world."

They approached a grand platform overlooking Aurelia. From here, Maya could see everything — the central plaza where people gathered for weekly events, the learning amphitheater where Solara hosted immersive workshops, the avatar customization temple where visitors chose identity layers aligned with their goals. "Every part of this world reflects who I am," Solara explained. "My values. My mission. My energy. My vision." Maya's eyes widened as she took it all in. She realized that Solara hadn't just built a brand. She had built a universe that embodied her essence. Visitors didn't just watch her content — they lived in her story. They participated in it. They became part of something bigger than themselves. And because of that, Solara's brand was unshakeable.

As they walked through the learning amphitheater, Solara waved her hand and the environment responded instantly. Holographic visuals appeared around them — lessons, concepts, animations, and stories that explained her mission. It wasn't a presentation. It was an experience. Maya felt herself drawn into the narrative as if the world itself were teaching her. "In the metaverse," Solara said gently, "your brand is not built on attention — it's built on immersion. People remember how you make them feel, not what you tell them. And immersive worlds allow you to shape emotions with sound, color, movement, architecture, and interaction."

They then entered the community courtyard where a group of avatars were discussing a new project. Some were mentors. Some were students. Some were brand-new visitors who had just discovered Aurelia that day. Yet all of them were collaborating, creating, brainstorming, and interacting as if they belonged. "This community is the heart of the brand," Solara whispered. "Not me. Not the content. The people. Their stories. Their contributions." Maya watched as avatars exchanged ideas, shared music, co-created art, and formed partnerships. She could feel the unity of the group — a sense of belonging that felt almost spiritual. She realized that in this world, everyone was both a participant and a co-creator. Solara had created a place where people didn't just follow her brand — they helped shape it. And that made it more powerful than any social media following could ever be.

As night fell in Aurelia, the world transformed. The sky shifted into a tapestry of stars, and bioluminescent plants glowed softly along the paths. Maya felt a deep sense of peace. She knew she wanted to build something like this — not a copy, but her own world, her own brand, her own experience. "How do I begin?" she asked quietly. Solara smiled. "By deciding what you want people to feel when they enter your world. Everything else grows from there." Maya nodded. It was so simple, yet so profound. She understood that the metaverse wasn't just a digital space — it was a canvas for identity, expression, community, and transformation. She felt her heart fill with inspiration, and for the first time in her career, she wasn't thinking about followers, algorithms, or branding tactics. She was thinking about worlds. Experiences. Emotions. Legacy. And she smiled, knowing that her journey into metaverse branding was only just beginning.

Chapter 2

Crafting Your Metaverse Identity: Avatars, Aesthetics & Brand Essence

Your metaverse identity is the foundation of your brand presence, influence, and authority across virtual worlds. While Web2 branding relied heavily on colors, fonts, logos, profile images, and curated feeds, the metaverse shifts identity into a three-dimensional, immersive, and emotionally expressive form. In this new environment, your avatar becomes your most powerful branding asset — a living representation of your mission, values, energy, and story. Your environment becomes an extension of your identity. Your voice, movements, style, and the world you build all contribute to how your audience perceives you. Chapter 2 will guide you through defining who you are in the metaverse, how to express it, and how to build the kind of identity people remember, trust, and gravitate toward.

The first element of crafting your metaverse identity is your **avatar**. Unlike a profile photo, an avatar is an active participant in your brand experience. It speaks, moves, interacts, teaches, entertains, and leads. Your avatar design should reflect your essence — whether you choose realism, stylization, minimalism, futurism, or symbolism. Some creators select avatars that mirror their real-world appearance to maintain authenticity. Others choose bold new personas that amplify the version of themselves they aspire to be. Your avatar's shape, colors, accessories, animations, and movement patterns all communicate personality traits. A coach may want a confident, grounded avatar with strong posture. A mindfulness instructor may opt for softness, fluidity, and calming aesthetics. A business strategist may choose clean, sharp, modern features. Every detail reinforces your message. In a world where first impressions occur in seconds, your avatar sets the emotional tone.

The second element is **aesthetic style** — the visual language your brand uses across worlds. In Web2, your color palette and design tone defined your identity. In the metaverse, aesthetics now include spatial themes, lighting, textures, soundscapes, architecture, avatar accessories, animations, and the emotional mood your environments create. A brand rooted in empowerment might use vibrant neon colors, bold holographic signage, and energetic music to drive motivation. A wellness brand may build nature-inspired environments with flowing water, soft lighting, and earthy tones. A creative brand may lean into surreal landscapes, dynamic geometries, or dream-like structures that stimulate imagination. Your aesthetic must be distinctive and recognizable, no matter where users encounter your brand — Decentraland, The

Sandbox, Spatial, VRChat, Meta Horizon, or future interconnected worlds. This consistency builds familiarity, trust, and memorability.

The third element is your **brand essence** — the underlying spirit that guides all experience design. Your brand essence is emotional, philosophical, and psychological. It defines how you want people to feel when they interact with you. It shapes the tone of your voice, the architecture of your world, the look of your avatar, and the design of your events. A brand whose essence is "transformation" will build worlds that feel like new beginnings. A brand whose essence is "connection" will design environments where collaboration is natural and comforting. A brand rooted in "challenge" may gamify environments to push users toward growth. Essence is more than mission statements; it's the emotional blueprint of your metaverse identity. When your essence is clear, everything you create feels coherent.

The fourth element is **identity consistency across platforms**. Metaverse worlds vary in design limitations, technological capabilities, avatar styles, and cultural communities. You may have one avatar in VRChat, another in Meta Horizon, and a voxel-style avatar in The Sandbox — yet your identity should remain recognizable across all. This requires a signature set of brand markers: consistent color motifs, signature accessories, iconic symbols, recognizable voice tone, and a stable emotional theme. The goal is to have users instantly recognize you, regardless of the world or avatar style. For example, anime creators, musicians, educators, coaches, and entrepreneurs who maintain consistent branding across worlds often build faster loyalty because audiences feel continuity across platforms.

The fifth element is **story-driven identity**. While visuals matter, storytelling is what turns an avatar into a meaningful presence. Your metaverse identity should include narrative elements that give your avatar purpose. Who are you in the metaverse? What is your role? What do you stand for? What journey do you offer your audience? Maybe your avatar is a guide leading people through transformation. Maybe you're a builder empowering others to create. Maybe you're a strategist opening doors to knowledge. Story adds depth, making your identity unforgettable and emotionally resonant. In a world filled with avatars, stories differentiate you more than design.

The sixth element is **emotional resonance**. People follow you not only for what you offer but for how you make them feel. Emotional branding in the metaverse is amplified through environmental design, avatar expression, interactive experiences, and vocal communication. A creator who cultivates warmth and support will attract audiences seeking safety and belonging. A high-energy trainer will attract ambitious achievers. A visionary strategist will attract future-focused thinkers. Emotional resonance determines who gravitates toward you, how long they stay, and how loyal they become. Your metaverse identity should be designed intentionally to evoke the emotional response that aligns with your mission.

The seventh element is **identity evolution**. Unlike traditional branding, which changes slowly, metaverse identities evolve dynamically. Your avatar may grow stronger over time. Your world may expand. New accessories, abilities, animations, and environments may reflect your growth. This evolution becomes part of your story and signals progress to your audience. It reinforces that your brand is alive. It encourages users to follow your journey. And it creates anticipation for what comes next. Identity evolution is one of the most powerful tools in the metaverse — one that allows your brand to feel organic, inspiring, and future-focused.

The final element of crafting your metaverse identity is **alignment** — the harmony between your avatar, world, aesthetic, voice, values, community experience, and offerings. When every element reinforces the same emotional and thematic signature, your brand becomes iconic. People instantly understand who you are, what you stand for, and why your world matters. This alignment sets the foundation for everything else you will build in the metaverse: your spaces, your business model, your events, your community, and your long-term digital legacy.

"Becoming Liora"

The mirror inside the Avatar Creation Temple shimmered with soft, warm light. Maya stood before it, her heart pounding with excitement. Solara had instructed her to return to Aurelia with a new identity — one that reflected her true essence. The room around her glowed with golden patterns that pulsed gently as if responding to her emotions. As she stepped closer to the mirror, the reflection flickered, showing not her earthly appearance, but a blank canvas — a glowing silhouette waiting to be shaped. She inhaled deeply. This was the moment she would become her metaverse self.

With a gentle gesture, Solara appeared beside her, her luminous form radiating calm wisdom. "This is where your journey begins," Solara told her. "Your avatar is more than a design. It is a projection of your inner world. It represents your mission and your future." The mirror's surface rippled like water, inviting Maya to touch it. As she did, her reflection transformed into a series of floating symbols — colors, shapes, textures, elemental patterns, and emotional signatures. Each symbol represented an aspect of her identity. Maya chose a soft teal glow to represent healing and clarity. She chose golden accents to symbolize guidance and empowerment. She chose crystalline patterns to represent transformation. As she made her selections, the avatar began to take shape.

Her new form materialized slowly — elegant, centered, glowing with soft energy, with eyes that radiated warmth and intelligence. The avatar was unmistakably her, yet elevated, refined, visionary. Solara smiled. "What will you name her?" Maya paused, feeling a surge of intuition. "Liora," she whispered. "It means light." Solara nodded. "Liora will carry your essence across worlds. Through her, people will feel your presence." Maya turned back toward the mirror, now seeing Liora standing before her — her posture confident, her colors radiant, her essence unmistakably aligned.

Solara led her into the Hall of Aesthetics, where endless gateways opened into different environment samples. They walked through worlds of every kind — lush forests, futuristic cities, serene oceans, celestial temples, floating libraries, and crystalline sanctuaries. Each world offered a different emotional atmosphere. "This is where your aesthetic language begins," Solara explained. "What emotional world do you want your audience to enter?" Maya stepped into a glowing meadow filled with floating blossoms. It was peaceful, uplifting, serene. Then she walked into a bold neon city where holograms swirled through the air with high intensity. It felt energized, fast-paced, and ambitious. She felt how each world changed her mood instantly. In the final chamber, she encountered an empty, customizable environment waiting to be shaped. She could feel her heart pulling her toward a blend of clarity and transformation — something peaceful, yet powerful. With Solara's guidance, she sketched luminous archways, gentle waterfalls, and floating platforms shaped like petals. She added golden pathways, teal blossoms, and soft glowing textures. As the world formed around her, Maya felt tears gather in her eyes. "This is you," Solara whispered. "Your essence in spatial form." It felt like stepping into a dream she didn't know she had. She sensed how visitors would feel when they entered — calm, inspired, capable, hopeful.

After they explored the new space, Solara brought her to the Circle of Stories, where creators defined the narrative of their identity. Maya stepped into the circle, and holographic symbols appeared around her — representing leadership, healing, innovation, courage, growth, and wisdom. She selected the symbols that resonated with her journey. As she activated them, a soft voice echoed through the chamber: "Who are you in the metaverse?" Maya closed her eyes. "I am Liora, a guide who helps others rise into their potential." The chamber responded with a soft glow, sealing her identity.

As they walked back toward Aurelia's central plaza, Liora's new form shimmering gently beside Solara, Maya felt an unfamiliar sense of alignment — as if part of her soul had settled into its rightful place. When they emerged into the gardens, avatars turned to look at her. Not at Maya... but at Liora. She felt her first moment of recognition. Not through status or followers, but through presence. Through essence. Through story. A young avatar approached her, smiling. "Your energy feels beautiful. Who are you?" Maya smiled softly. "I'm Liora."

That night, as Liora stood on a floating balcony overlooking the luminous world, she understood what Solara meant about identity. In the metaverse, you do not hide behind a brand. You step into it. You become it. And she knew, deep in her spirit, that her journey was only beginning — and that her new identity would open doors she could not yet imagine.

Chapter 3

Building Your Metaverse Headquarters: Worlds, Spaces, and Interactive Brand Environments

In the metaverse, your headquarters is the central hub of your identity — the place where your audience experiences your brand, interacts with you, connects with your community, and participates in your story. Unlike a website, which is flat and informational, a metaverse headquarters is fully immersive, spatial, emotional, and alive. It functions as a business center, a classroom, an event space, a community forum, a showroom, and a storytelling environment. The architecture, layout, lighting, sound, and interactive elements all shape the way people feel when they enter your world. Creating a compelling headquarters is one of the most powerful steps you can take to establish your metaverse brand, because it transforms your audience from passive observers into active participants within your digital universe.

The first principle of designing your metaverse headquarters is **alignment** — ensuring the world reflects your brand essence. In Web2 branding, people connect to your visuals; in Web3 branding, they connect to your environment. Your headquarters must express your identity instantly through its aesthetic language. A mindset coach might choose floating platforms, crystalline structures, and uplifting sound design to evoke transformation. A business strategist may prefer a futuristic tower with holographic data panels and clean geometric architecture to represent clarity and action. A wellness brand may design a sanctuary filled with waterfalls, soft textures, and natural lighting to promote emotional calm. Your world should feel like a place your audience immediately recognizes as yours — a digital home that expresses who you are without a single word spoken.

The second principle is **functionality** — creating practical areas within the world that support your brand's activities. Your headquarters may include an entrance plaza, welcome chamber, main hall, auditorium, breakout rooms, product showcases, coaching spaces, exhibition galleries, community hubs, a media center, and even interactive experiences such as gamified challenges or quests. Each space has a role. The entrance sets the emotional tone. The main hall serves as your central gathering area. The auditorium becomes the setting for your events and workshops. The community hub facilitates conversation and networking. The showroom presents your digital products, NFTs, merchandise, and collections. You can also include private coaching environments, mastermind lounges, office suites, and meditation areas depending on your brand's mission. The more intentional each space is, the more immersive and functional your headquarters becomes.

The third principle is **interactivity**, which transforms your headquarters from a static environment into a living experience. Interactivity can include clickable objects, animated elements, sound-reactive architecture, dynamic lighting, teleportation portals, gamified tasks, rewards systems, or guided holographic tutorials. For example, a fitness coach may include a virtual workout arena where avatars can practice movements. A business mentor may add an interactive goal-setting module where users walk through their roadmap. A musician may place playable instruments or sound pads throughout the world. A real estate educator may allow users to explore modeled homes or investment simulations. Interactivity creates engagement, deepens connection, and increases retention — the more your audience can do inside the space, the more likely they are to stay, return, and explore.

The fourth principle is **flow** — designing your environment so that users intuitively know where to go and what to do next. A well-designed headquarters guides them naturally from one experience to another. This involves strategic layout, lighting contrast, environmental cues, symbolic pathways, and intentional user journey mapping. If you want visitors to begin with a welcome orientation, the entrance should lead gently into that area. If you want them to attend events, the architecture should subtly pull them toward the auditorium. If you want them to see your product offerings, you can place interactive showcases along the main pathways. Good flow makes your world feel magical, seamless, and emotionally satisfying.

The fifth principle is **identity expression through architecture**. In the metaverse, building design is part of your story. The shapes, materials, symmetry, layout, and movement patterns all communicate meaning. Circular structures represent unity and flow. Angular structures communicate precision and strategy. Floating islands express freedom. Transparent materials symbolize openness. Warm colors feel inviting; cool colors feel sophisticated; neons feel energetic. Your world becomes a storytelling tool, shaping the emotional narrative your audience experiences. Architecture becomes language — a language your brand speaks fluently when designed intentionally.

The sixth principle is **scalability**. A metaverse headquarters isn't static. It must be able to grow alongside your brand. You may start with a small three-room environment — a welcome chamber, a classroom, and a community area. As your following expands, you can add more structures: a conference center, an onboarding portal, a shop, private coaching chambers, collaborative studios, or even entire floating districts dedicated to specialized experiences. Your headquarters should evolve as your business evolves. This creates anticipation within your community and strengthens their sense of belonging as they watch your world expand.

The seventh principle is **accessibility**. A metaverse headquarters should be simple to access even for people who are new to Web3. Entry portals should be intuitive. Navigation should be beginner-friendly. Clear instructions or a welcome guide can help users move through the world. The technology should not overwhelm newcomers. You may consider offering both a complex main headquarters and a simplified, lightweight version for mobile or browser users. Accessibility ensures your brand remains inclusive and welcoming for all.

The final principle is **emotion** – the overall feeling your world gives to visitors. This feeling becomes the heart of your brand presence. Whether you aim to evoke inspiration, excitement, grounding, creativity, empowerment, wisdom, or serenity, your headquarters allows you to engineer that emotional response intentionally. People will return to your world not because of logic, but because of how it makes them feel. Emotion is the gravitational force of metaverse branding. Design your headquarters around the emotions that support your mission, and your brand will become a world people never want to leave.

"The Birth of Liora's Sanctuary"

The platform materialized beneath her feet, glowing softly with teal and gold. Liora — Maya's metaverse self — stood at the edge of a blank expanse floating high above Aurelia's shimmering skyline. The air hummed with possibility. This floating island, Solara had told her, would become her headquarters — the place where her journey as a creator truly began. All around her, the world was a blank canvas, waiting for her to shape it with intention.

Solara appeared beside her, a warm light illuminating the space around her. "This is where you create the heart of your brand," she said gently. "Your sanctuary. Your headquarters. Your world." Liora took a slow breath, feeling the weight and excitement of the moment. She looked across the empty sky, knowing that within minutes or hours it could transform into something vibrant, meaningful, and alive. The thought electrified her.

She lifted her hand, and the air responded. A soft vibration pulsed through the platform, and a golden circle appeared beneath her feet. "Begin with essence," Solara reminded her. "What do you want people to feel when they enter your world?" Liora closed her eyes. She envisioned peace, transformation, clarity, and rising into potential. As the emotions flowed through her mind, the space responded – glowing teal mist swirled into the air, forming gentle pathways that curved outward like petals. Crystalline structures began to rise from the ground, soft and translucent, reflecting hints of gold. A waterfall formed along the far edge, floating gently in midair, its water cascading into nothingness.

"This is beautiful," Liora whispered, watching her sanctuary come alive. Solara nodded. "Your essence is clear. This world reflects you." They walked along the forming pathways, and as Liora stepped across the teal-glowing surface, more of the environment materialized: floating blossoms, soft ambient music, gentle particles drifting like fireflies. The world felt serene yet powerful – exactly what she had envisioned. For the first time, Liora sensed what it meant to create not just a space, but a feeling.

They approached an empty circular platform at the center. "This will be your main hall," Solara said. "Design it with intention. This is where your community will gather." Liora focused her thoughts, and the ground transformed. A luminous dome rose around them, its walls made of shimmering glass-like material. Golden patterns danced across the surface like constellations. A soft light radiated from above. The room felt sacred. Inviting. Safe. Liora imagined leading her first gathering here, speaking to her community from the center of the dome, guiding them through transformation. Next, she created her auditorium — a floating amphitheater with layered platforms that allowed everyone to see her clearly. Golden beams flowed along the edges of each level, and gentle luminescent threads connected the seats, symbolizing unity. She imagined teaching workshops here, hosting events, bringing her community together. The structure made her feel powerful yet grounded.

Solara led her toward the edge of the sanctuary, where Liora envisioned a collection of smaller chambers connected by floating bridges. "These will be your coaching suites," she explained. "Private spaces for deeper conversations." Each chamber appeared with a different emotional tone — one deeply calming, another empowering, another reflective. She envisioned hosting personal sessions here, guiding individuals through breakthroughs.

As they walked further, the sanctuary began to feel alive. Crystalline plants swayed gently, waterfalls sparkled in the golden light, and floating lanterns drifted through the air. Liora realized she was building not just a headquarters, but a refuge — a world where people could find clarity, hope, and transformation. She stepped into the community garden she had designed — an open space with circular seating, blossoming trees, and small glowing ponds. She imagined her audience gathering there after events, forming friendships, supporting one another, building community. It filled her with warmth.

Finally, Solara brought her to a large empty expanse near the back of the sanctuary. “This space,” Solara said softly, “is for the part of your story you haven’t discovered yet.” Liora felt a thrill of possibility as she looked out over the open sky. She didn’t know what this area would become — but she knew it would evolve as she grew. “Leave room for your future,” Solara whispered. “Your world will expand as you do.”

As night fell over Aurelia, the sanctuary glowed softly with teal and gold. Liora stood at the center, overwhelmed with pride. She had built something that reflected her spirit — not a logo, not a brand identity in the traditional sense, but a living world. A home. A beacon for every person she would guide. She looked at Solara, gratitude radiating through her avatar. “This feels like the beginning of everything,” she said.

Solara smiled. “It is.”

And as Liora gazed across her sanctuary — the waterfalls, the glowing gardens, the rising towers of light — she knew she had taken her first true step into becoming a creator whose presence would echo across worlds.

Chapter 4

Designing Metaverse Experiences: Events, Workshops, Gatherings, and Immersive Encounters

Designing metaverse experiences is the core of transforming your brand from a static presence into a living ecosystem. The metaverse gives creators, coaches, and businesses the ability to host gatherings that feel personal, memorable, and emotionally powerful. Unlike traditional webinars or livestreams, metaverse experiences engage all senses: visual immersion, spatial presence, environmental responsiveness, avatar interaction, and real-time co-creation. These experiences deepen trust, strengthen community bonds, and allow your audience to participate rather than simply observe. When done correctly, your events become transformational moments inside your world — moments that people talk about, return to, and associate permanently with your brand.

The first principle of designing metaverse experiences is **intentional emotional architecture** — shaping the feelings you want participants to experience. In the metaverse, emotion is engineered through environment, lighting, sound, spatial layout, pacing, avatar animation, and interactive elements. For example, a breakthrough coaching workshop may be held inside an ascension-themed amphitheater with rising platforms and uplifting music. A business strategy session may take place inside a clean, structured room with holographic screens and data displays. A community celebration may happen in a vibrant plaza with dynamic lighting and animated decorations. Every event begins with defining the emotional journey: calm, inspired, energized, connected, transformed, curious, or empowered. Once the emotional target is clear, the environment can be shaped to support it.

The second principle is **experience flow** – guiding users through a structured sequence of moments. A powerful metaverse event typically includes a welcoming phase, an orientation phase, a core experience phase, an interactive engagement phase, and a closing integration phase. The welcoming phase sets the emotional tone as avatars enter the space. The orientation phase ensures newcomers understand how to navigate the environment. The core experience phase delivers your main content, whether teaching, storytelling, coaching, performing, or demonstrating. The engagement phase allows participants to interact, practice skills, or collaborate in real time. The closing phase reinforces the lesson, emotional shift, or call to action. This structured flow creates coherence and helps participants feel guided throughout the event.

The third principle is **interactivity**, which differentiates metaverse events from traditional digital experiences. Interactivity can include live Q&A in avatar form, group activities, breakout rooms, object interaction, collaborative building, gamified challenges, teleportation sequences, reward-based tasks, or guided movement experiences. You can ask participants to walk through symbolic portals, follow guided journeys, place objects in specific areas, activate holographic modules, or navigate spatial puzzles. Interactivity increases engagement, emotional impact, and memory retention. When participants actively do something inside your world, their brains store the experience as a lived moment rather than a passive observation.

The fourth principle is **immersion** — the feeling of presence that makes experiences unforgettable. Immersion comes from carefully integrating soundscapes, visual cues, spatial depth, avatar proximity, lighting changes, environmental effects, and real-time responses. For example, when teaching a breakthrough moment, the lighting may brighten gradually as the lesson builds. When guiding meditation, the environment may shift into softer tones with slow-moving visual elements. When celebrating milestones, fireworks or particle effects may trigger from the sky. The more dynamic and responsive your environment, the deeper the immersion. Immersion makes your events feel magical — transportive — and more impactful than traditional digital interactions.

The fifth principle is **participation**, which transforms audience members into contributors. A well-designed metaverse experience encourages the community to help shape the event. Participants may share insights in real time, decorate spaces collaboratively, co-create art, build symbolic structures, vote on environmental changes, or add energy flows to the world through movements or animations. Participation strengthens belonging. It turns spectators into co-creators. As people contribute, they emotionally invest in the world — and in your brand.

The sixth principle is **transformation** — creating experiences that leave lasting impact. Some events simply entertain; powerful metaverse experiences transform. Transformation may come from guided lessons, emotional breakthroughs, collaborative accomplishments, symbolic rituals, immersive storytelling, or clarity-producing exercises. When someone enters your event feeling one way and leaves feeling elevated, empowered, or renewed, your brand becomes permanently anchored in their memory. Transformation is the currency of metaverse branding — the driving force behind loyalty and long-term community growth. The seventh principle is **scalability and repetition**. A well-designed event can be repeated for new audiences, scaled into larger gatherings, adapted into multiple worlds, or transformed into automated experiences led by AI guides or pre-programmed sequences. You can host weekly immersive gatherings, monthly community events, annual conferences, themed ceremonies, training academies, product launches, and multi-stage experiences. Over time, your events become rituals — experiences that your community anticipates and returns to. Ritualized experiences strengthen culture and increase brand gravity.

The final principle is **integration** — ensuring that the experience participants have in your event becomes part of your larger brand ecosystem. After an event, your world should guide them toward next steps: joining your community hub, exploring your sanctuary, taking a course, participating in a program, purchasing a digital asset, or attending another gathering. Integration ensures your experiences build momentum rather than ending abruptly. The best metaverse brands design experiences that echo long after the event ends, with participants feeling connected to the world and eager to return.

"The First Gathering in the Sanctuary"

The sky above Liora's sanctuary shimmered with golden twilight as the gates opened for the first time. Liora stood at the entrance of her new world, her teal and gold avatar glowing softly beneath the floating lanterns. This was the moment she had been preparing for — her first gathering, her first event, her first opportunity to share her sanctuary with others. She inhaled deeply, feeling a mix of nervousness and excitement. Solara stood beside her, radiating calm support. "They're ready," Solara whispered. "And so are you."

One by one, avatars began to materialize along the entrance platform. Some appeared in flashes of light, others as swirling particles before forming fully. Their footsteps echoed gently as they gazed around with awe. Liora watched their reactions — the widening eyes, the soft gasps, the quiet smiles — and her heart swelled. They were experiencing her essence, her energy, her world. Solara stepped forward, her voice carrying through the air like music. "Welcome to Liora's Sanctuary," she announced. "Tonight, you embark on a journey inside a world built with intention, heart, and purpose."

Liora led them down the glowing pathways toward the Main Hall. As the group entered the luminous dome, the walls shifted subtly to teal and gold hues, responding to their presence. The light grew warmer. The soundscape softened into a gentle harmonic hum. The avatars gathered in a circular formation around Liora, who stood at the center, feeling the weight of the moment. She raised her hand and the room quieted. "Thank you for being here," she said. "This sanctuary was created for you — a place for clarity, growth, and transformation." Her voice felt steady. Confident. True.

She guided the participants through a grounding exercise, inviting them to breathe in harmony with the rising and falling glow of the room. As they synced, the dome brightened slightly, reflecting the collective energy. Then she led them to the Ascension Hall — a floating amphitheater with layered platforms. As the group moved along the pathways, the sky shifted into luminous purples and blues, stars twinkling overhead. When they arrived, the amphitheater came alive. Golden lines traced along its edges, and a soft wind swirled, signaling the beginning.

Liora began her workshop, teaching key principles of clarity and purpose. As she spoke, holographic illustrations materialized around the space — flowing diagrams, symbolic patterns, and gentle animations that brought her lessons to life. Participants leaned in, mesmerized. The amphitheater shifted subtly as the lesson deepened: lighting brightened during moments of empowerment, softened during moments of reflection, and expanded outward when Liora guided them through breakthrough visualizations. It felt like the space itself was collaborating with her — responding to her words, amplifying her energy. Then came the interactive portion of the experience. Liora gestured toward a crystal pathway that extended into the sky. “Follow me,” she said. As avatars stepped onto the path, it lit up with each footstep. They walked upward toward a floating platform called the Clarity Gate. Here, Liora guided them through a symbolic gesture: placing a glowing orb — representing an old belief — into a shimmering pool at the platform’s center. As each participant released their orb, the pool glowed brighter and the sky shifted. It was subtle, but powerful. People were letting go of something — and the world responded.

Afterward, she led them to the Community Garden where soft music played and floating blossoms drifted through the air. Participants gathered into small groups, sharing insights, encouraging each other, offering reflections. Liora watched as connections formed — not through forced networking, but through authentic shared experience. Solara appeared at her side. “This is how a community begins,” she whispered.

The event closed inside the Main Hall, where the lights dimmed into a soft evening glow. Liora thanked everyone for being part of her first gathering. Many avatars approached her, expressing gratitude and excitement. “Your sanctuary is magical," one said. "I felt something shift inside me," another whispered. Their words warmed her spirit.

As the last avatars departed, Liora walked alone along the glowing pathway overlooking the sanctuary. The sky sparkled with distant stars and soft teal blossoms drifted past her gently. She felt changed — expanded — as if tonight had awakened a new chapter in her journey. Solara appeared beside her once more. "You did beautifully," she said. "Your world is alive now. And tonight, you didn't just host an event. You created transformation."

Liora gazed across her sanctuary, her heart full. She knew this was only the beginning — and that the experiences she would create in the future would shape countless journeys. For the first time, she truly felt like a creator of worlds.

Chapter 5

Building Community in the Metaverse: Culture, Connection & Long-Term Engagement

A brand in the metaverse is only as strong as the community that gathers around it. While Web2 communities form in comment sections, group chats, and social media threads, metaverse communities form through *shared presence, shared emotion*, and *shared experiences* inside immersive worlds. They don't just follow your brand; they inhabit it. Community members become friends, collaborators, supporters, and advocates. They return not because of algorithms but because your world feels like home. In Web3, community is not a marketing tactic — it is the foundation of your brand ecosystem. Chapter 5 will teach you how to build a community that is loyal, active, connected, and invested in your metaverse identity for years to come.

The first principle of building community in the metaverse is **creating a shared emotional culture**. The emotional tone of your world becomes its cultural DNA. Are you creating a brand built on empowerment, transformation, curiosity, adventure, creativity, or serenity? Every decision — from your avatar's tone to your world's lighting — shapes the emotional culture people feel when they arrive. Culture is not rules; it is energy. A strong metaverse community has a unified emotional signature that people instantly sense. When your culture is clear, it attracts people who resonate with it. When your emotional environment is consistent, people return to experience it again and again.

The second principle is **structure and accessibility**. A thriving community requires clear spaces, roles, rituals, and gathering points. Inside your headquarters, members should know where to meet, where conversations happen, and where new visitors begin. Welcoming areas, orientation portals, mission statements, community plazas, and teaching spaces help people feel grounded. Accessibility is crucial: newcomers must feel safe, guided, and supported. Clear navigation signs, friendly onboarding sessions, or AI welcome assistants help ease the learning curve. When you provide structure, the community feels organized rather than chaotic — and people stay longer because they know how to participate.

The third principle is **meaningful participation**. Community is built through action, not observation. The metaverse gives you unique tools to help members participate deeply: collaborative building, group quests, co-creation sessions, brainstorming workshops, mindfulness gatherings, shared rituals, avatar challenges, voting events, token-gated activities, or interactive storytelling. When members contribute to the growth of your world, they feel ownership. Ownership creates loyalty. Participation transforms visitors into members, members into leaders, and leaders into ambassadors who spread your brand across worlds.

The fourth principle is **social bonding** – helping members form genuine relationships with each other. People stay in communities because of the humans they connect with, not the brand alone. Create spaces where natural interaction happens: communal gardens, lounges, fireside areas, walking paths, meditation groves, scenic overlooks, or virtual cafés. Small groups should be encouraged to form around shared interests – learning, creativity, business, wellness, crypto, gaming, storytelling, and more. Host bonding events such as avatar interviews, group journeys, reflective circles, and collaboration nights. When members bond with each other, the community becomes self-sustaining.

The fifth principle is **recognition and leadership pathways**. Every strong community needs leaders – not authoritarian leaders, but facilitators who help nurture culture. Recognize members who participate often, help newcomers, or embody your brand's values. Give them titles, badges, roles, or special areas within your world. Allow them to host their own small gatherings or co-lead events. When members rise into leadership roles, the community expands organically without you carrying the entire burden. Leadership pathways strengthen loyalty and give your community resilience, stability, and identity.

The sixth principle is **community storytelling**. A community becomes powerful when its members feel part of a shared narrative. Celebrate milestones, breakthroughs, contributions, and events. Share community lore — stories of how the world was created, why it exists, and who plays key roles within it. Let members help build that story. Storytelling creates meaning. Meaning creates belonging. Belonging creates longevity. A metaverse brand with strong narrative roots becomes more than a space — it becomes a world with history, purpose, and soul.

The seventh principle is **rituals and consistency**. Rituals create rhythm and give your community emotional anchors. Weekly gatherings, monthly ceremonies, seasonal festivals, avatar transformation nights, meditations, goal-setting circles, celebrations, and immersive learning events — all these give members something to look forward to. Consistent rituals train your community to return. Rituals create culture. Culture creates identity. Identity creates growth. The final principle is **long-term engagement through transformation**. People remain in communities that help them grow. If your world facilitates transformation — emotional, intellectual, creative, or professional — members feel connected to the journey and remain for years. Transformation is the glue of metaverse branding. Through immersive events, personal breakthroughs, meaningful relationships, and shared experiences, your community transforms together. When you become the architect of their transformation, they become the long-term guardians of your world.

"A Community Awakens"

A gentle morning glow filled the sanctuary as Liora walked along the floating pathways, preparing for her next great milestone. Today wasn't a workshop or a training — it was the first community gathering meant not for teaching, but for connection. Solara's words echoed through her mind: *"Your world will become a home when your people find each other."* Liora had created her sanctuary with purpose. Now it was time to invite others not just to listen — but to *belong*.

Avatars began to appear one by one, stepping through the golden portal with curiosity in their eyes. Some she recognized from her earlier workshops. Others were new travelers drawn by whispers of her world. They gathered at the entrance plaza, gazing at the glowing blossoms and shimmering teal pathways. Liora approached them slowly, her avatar emitting a warm, inviting glow. "Welcome back," she said softly. "Today, we explore not just the sanctuary — but each other."

She guided them to the Community Garden, which had transformed since their last visit. Floating lanterns drifted gently overhead. Crystalline benches lined the pathways. Soft music hummed in the background, shaping the air with warmth. The avatars formed a loose circle around Liora. She began the gathering not with a lecture, but with a question: "What brought you here?" At first, there was silence. Then, one by one, voices rose.

A healer spoke of longing for a space where people understood her purpose. A student described searching for guidance during a confusing season. A creator explained that he wanted to build something meaningful but felt lost. As each avatar shared their story, the room shifted subtly — the lighting warmed, the blossoms brightened, and the atmosphere thickened with emotion. Liora listened intently, feeling the sacredness of their vulnerability. She realized that a community wasn't built through content. It was built through truth.

She invited them to walk with her toward the Reflection Grove — a quiet grove surrounded by tall, luminous trees that emitted a soft teal glow. Here, avatars naturally split into smaller groups, sitting together beneath the radiant foliage. Liora watched as conversations blossomed. Avatars who were once strangers laughed together. Others shared fears, dreams, and ideas. A pair of creators began discussing a collaborative project. Two healers exchanged wisdom. A strategist offered advice to a newcomer. It was happening — the community was awakening, forming bonds that stretched beyond her individual influence.

Solara appeared at the edge of the grove, watching with a wistful smile. "They're weaving themselves together," she whispered. Liora approached her mentor. "I didn't expect it to feel like this," she said. "It's as if the sanctuary is responding to them." Solara nodded. "A world becomes whole when its people breathe life into it. You created the space. They are creating the spirit."

Later, Liora led them on a journey through the sanctuary, stopping at each symbolic location. In the Ascension Hall, she encouraged them to speak the goals they were committed to pursuing. As each avatar voiced their intention, golden lights flickered around the amphitheater. In the Clarity Gate, she asked them to release a fear that held them back. When they placed their glowing orbs into the pool, the water shimmered like stardust, absorbing their burdens. In the Plaza of Echoes, she invited them to leave behind a message for future visitors.

Holographic inscriptions floated into the air — words of encouragement, gratitude, wisdom, and hope.

As night settled, Liora guided them to the Sanctuary Summit — the highest platform overlooking the entire world. Dozens of avatars gathered, their glowing forms reflecting off the tranquil sky. They stood together in silence, watching the sanctuary come alive with starlight. It was a breathtaking sight. Liora stepped forward and spoke softly. "You are not just visitors in this sanctuary. You are its first guardians, its first storytellers, its first community. This world is yours as much as it is mine."

A gentle breeze flowed through the air, and for a moment, no one spoke. Then an avatar placed a hand on Liora's shoulder. "Thank you," they whispered. "I've never felt this connected in any digital space." Others echoed the sentiment. Liora felt her chest warm with emotion. She had dreamed of building a sanctuary; she had never imagined it would become a family.

As the avatars slowly departed that night, leaving trails of light behind them, Liora stood alone at the summit, gazing at the world she had built — now filled with voices, memories, and shared moments. Solara appeared beside her, her presence glowing like a gentle flame. "Your community has begun," she said. "Protect it. Nurture it. Let it evolve."

Liora nodded, knowing this was the beginning of something greater than her brand, greater than her sanctuary – something alive, growing, and capable of shaping countless journeys. A community had awakened, and with it, the true spirit of her world.

Chapter 6

Monetizing Your Metaverse Brand: Products, Services, NFTs, Memberships & Digital Assets

Monetization in the metaverse represents a powerful evolution of the creator economy. Instead of offering only traditional services or digital products, you gain access to entirely new revenue streams that combine identity, immersion, interactivity, and ownership. In the metaverse, you can sell experiences, access, environments, collectibles, avatar enhancements, tokenized memberships, virtual real estate, AI-powered guides, and community-driven assets. This chapter will show you how to build sustainable and scalable monetization systems that align with your brand, your community values, and your long-term vision.

The first principle of monetizing your metaverse brand is **value clarity** — knowing what transformation, experience, or benefit your brand delivers. People don't buy products; they buy outcomes, emotions, identity expression, and access to worlds that enhance their lives. Before creating your monetization structure, define the core value your brand offers: transformation, knowledge, community, entertainment, empowerment, creativity, or personal growth. Once your core value is clear, every product and service you design can reinforce and amplify that value. Your monetization should feel like a natural extension of your identity – not a forced add-on.

The second principle is **offer architecture** – designing a structured ecosystem of products at different levels of accessibility. Entry-level offers may include inexpensive NFTs, avatar accessories, basic workshops, or casual experiences. Mid-level offers may include immersive courses, coaching sessions, membership tiers, token-gated events, or interactive environments. High-level offers may involve exclusive masterminds, private mentorship, custom worlds, branded digital real estate, or advanced immersive programs. A complete offer ecosystem ensures your world appeals to newcomers, enthusiasts, and serious participants alike. It also creates elegant pathways for members to ascend into deeper levels of your brand.

The third principle is **experience-based monetization**. The metaverse is uniquely positioned to monetize through immersive experiences that would be impossible in traditional digital spaces. These include interactive workshops, guided journeys, meditations, performances, gamified quests, avatar challenges, ceremonial gatherings, multi-world adventures, and transformational experiences. Unlike a webinar or video course, a metaverse experience is something people *live*, not just watch. This makes them more valuable — and more desirable. People will pay premium prices for experiences that change how they feel, what they believe, or how they see themselves.

The fourth principle is **NFT-based monetization**, which introduces digital ownership into your brand ecosystem. NFTs can represent access passes, membership tiers, digital collectibles, avatar skins, virtual tools, interactive objects, symbolic artifacts, or commemorative items tied to your story. They can be used to manage subscriptions, reward engagement, or offer lifetime access. The power of NFTs lies in their ability to offer ownership, exclusivity, provenance, and resale potential. Members can trade, gift, or sell them — creating a secondary economy around your brand. When designed thoughtfully, NFTs can deepen connection and reward loyalty rather than feeling speculative.

The fifth principle is **token-gated communities**, which allow you to create exclusive spaces accessible only to members who hold specific NFTs or digital assets. Token-gated worlds elevate your brand from basic content delivery into premium community membership. These spaces can include private lounges, mastermind rooms, collaboration hubs, advanced training portals, or special events. Token-gating adds value through exclusivity, status, and access to high-level opportunities. When done well, token-gated spaces become aspirational — motivating members to engage more deeply with your brand.

The sixth principle is **virtual merchandise and avatar enhancements**. People in the metaverse invest heavily in their digital appearance and self-expression. You can offer avatar clothing, accessories, effects, emotes, animations, symbolic items, or tools aligned with your brand's identity. A wellness brand may sell glowing meditation orbs or nature-inspired wings. A strategist may sell holographic tools or futuristic gear. A creativity brand may offer surreal accessories or artistic visual effects. Because avatars represent identity, people are willing to pay for digital items that align them with your brand narrative.

The seventh principle is **subscription-based and membership-based models**. Monthly or annual memberships can provide ongoing access to experiences, events, environments, coaching, or exclusive content. Metaverse memberships feel more valuable than Web2 memberships because they are spatial, interactive, and social. Members don't just unlock content — they unlock a place where they belong. Membership tiers can include access to special areas, exclusive avatars, private gatherings, reward systems, or early access to new worlds. Subscriptions create predictable income while offering your community continuity.

The eighth principle is **service-based monetization**, which uses metaverse environments to enhance coaching, consulting, mentoring, teaching, or creative services. You can host high-ticket coaching sessions inside private world chambers, deliver training through immersive presentations, conduct group strategy sessions inside holographic boardrooms, or run creative workshops inside interactive studios. Metaverse services feel more premium and can justify higher pricing because they are immersive and personalized.

The final principle is **ecosystem expansion**, where multiple monetization methods work together to create a long-term digital economy around your brand. A well-designed brand ecosystem might include NFTs for access, memberships for ongoing engagement, immersive experiences for transformation, merchandise for identity expression, consulting or coaching for high-level support, and digital real estate for large-scale experiences. Over time, your monetization structure becomes a thriving digital economy supported by your community. When designed with integrity, creativity, and alignment, this ecosystem becomes sustainable, scalable, and profitable for years to come.

"The Gift of the Golden Orbit"

The sanctuary glowed with soft evening light as Liora prepared for one of the most meaningful moments of her journey – offering her first digital artifact, a symbolic object designed to deepen her community's connection to her world. She called it the *Golden Orbit*, a radiant orb infused with swirling patterns of teal and gold. It represented clarity, transformation, and the promise of inner illumination. Tonight, she would reveal it for the first time.

Avatars gathered in the Main Hall, their forms illuminated by the gentle light that reflected off the crystalline dome. The air felt charged with anticipation. Liora appeared on the central platform, her avatar shimmering with a soft golden glow. "Thank you all for coming," she said warmly. "Tonight, I want to share something that carries the essence of our sanctuary. Something you can take with you wherever you travel in the metaverse."

She lifted her hand, and a soft pulse of light radiated outward. In an instant, the Golden Orbit appeared at the center of the room – a gently floating sphere emitting delicate trails of light. Gasps echoed through the dome as avatars stepped closer, mesmerized by its beauty. The orb responded to their presence, glowing brighter as the community gathered around it. Liora watched their faces, feeling a warm surge of connection. This wasn't just a digital item. It was a representation of her world, her mission, her heart.

Solara stepped forward, her glowing form reflecting the orb's light. "Artifacts like these carry meaning," she said gently. "They remind us of who we are becoming." The room grew quiet. Liora felt her energy center. "The Golden Orbit is not simply an object," she explained. "It is a symbol of your journey — a reminder of your power to grow, transform, and illuminate your path. It unlocks new areas of the sanctuary, gives you access to exclusive gatherings, and serves as a tool for future experiences."

The avatars exchanged glances, excitement building. Liora smiled deeply. "Tonight, each of you will receive one." A wave of shimmering energy rippled across the room. One by one, Golden Orbits appeared in the hands of the gathered avatars. Their forms glowed as they held the orbs — some lifting them with reverence, others examining them with curiosity. A healer whispered, "I can feel its energy." A creator smiled, saying, "It's like holding a piece of the sanctuary."

Liora watched as each avatar bonded with their orb. Some placed it into their chest, merging it with their avatar's heart space. Others let it orbit around them like a companion. The orbs adjusted to each person's energy, glowing at different intensities and displaying unique patterns. It was beautiful to witness. The sanctuary responded with subtle pulses of light, as if welcoming the beginning of a new era.

Solara guided them toward the Chamber of Echoes — a space newly created for this moment. Inside, the walls shimmered with swirling patterns, and the air felt electric. "This chamber," Solara said, "was designed to activate your Golden Orbits." When participants stepped inside, their orbs floated into the air, aligning with the chamber's energy. Suddenly, beams of light connected the orbs in a constellation of glowing pathways. The community gasped as the chamber filled with radiant interconnection.

Liora spoke softly, her voice echoing through the room. "This is our unity. This is our story. Each of your orbs carries a piece of our sanctuary, and together, they illuminate this world." She watched as avatars reached out toward the beams of light, feeling the energy pass through them. The chamber vibrated with a resonance that made Liora's heart swell. This was more than a product offering — it was a shared experience, a moment of meaning.

After the activation, the group gathered in the Community Garden, their orbs softly glowing around them. Some avatars reflected on what the gift meant to them. Others discussed ideas for future creations. A few expressed gratitude with tears shimmering in their digital eyes. Liora felt humbled. She had hoped the Golden Orbit would bring them closer; she hadn't anticipated how profoundly it would bond them to each other.

When the gathering ended and the avatars departed, Liora walked alone through the gardens, the moonlit sky reflecting off the glowing water. Her own Golden Orbit floated gently beside her, pulsing softly with her breath. Solara appeared once more, radiating pride. "You've given them more than a gift," she said. "You've offered them belonging."

Liora looked up at the sky, feeling the weight and wonder of the moment. She knew her sanctuary had just entered a new chapter — not as a world to visit, but as an economy, an ecosystem, and a home where meaning and value could grow. The Golden Orbit wasn't just the first monetized offering of her brand. It was the first heartbeat of a living digital legacy.

Chapter 7

Scaling Your Metaverse Brand: Automation, AI Integration, Partnerships & World Expansion

Scaling a metaverse brand requires a different mindset than scaling a traditional business. In Web2, scaling meant increasing content output, running more ads, building larger email lists, or expanding social media presence. In the metaverse, scaling happens inside *worlds*, *experiences*, and *ecosystems*. It's about growing your influence through space, connection, technology, and collaboration. Your world becomes the central hub of your digital empire, and scaling that world means expanding its architecture, automating key functions, empowering leaders, forming strategic partnerships, and integrating AI-driven systems that allow your brand to operate even when you're offline. Scaling turns your metaverse identity from a personal project into a self-sustaining universe.

The first principle of scaling your metaverse brand is **world expansion** – adding new areas, districts, experiences, and interactive layers to your headquarters. As your community grows, they will naturally explore deeper territories of your world. Expansion can include advanced training wings, specialized areas for different community groups, creative studios, virtual shops, multi-level sanctuaries, themed arenas, ceremonial chambers, collaboration districts, meditation gardens, or adventure pathways. Expansion is not just about making your world bigger — it's about making it *richer*. Each new area should serve a purpose: transformation, education, creativity, empowerment, or community bonding. When done intentionally, expansion reinforces your brand story while giving your audience new levels of immersion and meaning.

The second principle is **automation**, which allows your brand to scale without overwhelming your time and energy. Automation in the metaverse includes AI-powered greeters who welcome newcomers, guided orientation avatars, automated onboarding pathways, pre-programmed holographic lessons, interactive tutorials, open-world quests, and AI mentors that teach foundational concepts. Automated experiences allow your community to explore your world at their own pace, independent of your schedule. Automation is not meant to replace your presence; it is meant to extend it — creating continuity for your community when you are unavailable. A well-designed automated system enhances engagement, reduces confusion, and keeps your brand active around the clock. The third principle is **AI integration**, which elevates your brand into the next era of digital business.

AI avatars can assist members, answer questions, guide visitors, analyze behavior, recommend experiences, and personalize journeys based on user preferences. AI-driven environments can adjust lighting, music, and interactivity based on emotional cues. Intelligent systems can track community progress, reward participation, unlock achievements, or deliver customized lessons. AI can also generate new content, environments, story elements, and even events dynamically. When AI becomes part of your world, your community receives a deeper, more adaptive experience — one that evolves with them. AI allows your world to feel alive, intuitive, responsive, and endlessly expansive.

The fourth principle is **leadership decentralization** — empowering members of your community to step into leadership roles. As your brand grows, you cannot host every event, manage every group, or lead every experience alone. Identify community members who embody your values, demonstrate consistency, and show natural leadership qualities. Offer them roles such as hosts, guides, mentors, moderators, event facilitators, or world guardians. Give them spaces to run their own gatherings. Let them contribute to world-building. Let them create themed zones within your world. Decentralization builds loyalty, strengthens culture, and distributes the weight of community nurturing across multiple hearts rather than one. The fifth principle is

partnerships, which unlock exponential growth. Strategic partnerships allow your world to connect with other creators, coaches, brands, influencers, educators, and communities. Partnerships can include co-hosted events, shared training grounds, collaborative quests, cross-world portals, joint NFT collections, co-branded spaces, and community exchanges. When two worlds connect, both communities expand. Your brand becomes part of a broader metaverse network rather than an isolated realm. Partnerships multiply visibility, credibility, and creative energy. The best partnerships are aligned with your mission and serve your community's growth.

The sixth principle is **ecosystem integration** – connecting all your monetization models, world features, AI systems, community spaces, and brand identity into one unified experience. Ecosystem integration ensures your world doesn't feel fragmented. Members should move seamlessly between events, training modules, NFT utilities, membership tiers, token-gated areas, quests, marketplaces, and community hubs. Every part of your world should feel interconnected and intentional. Integration strengthens retention because members always know where to go, what to do, and how to grow inside your world. When your ecosystem is cohesive, your world becomes addictive – a place people return to daily.

The seventh principle is **expanding your reach across multiple platforms**. Your metaverse brand should not live on one world alone. It should operate across multiple universes: Decentraland, Spatial, Meta Horizon, VRChat, The Sandbox, or new emerging platforms. Each platform attracts different demographics, aesthetics, and community cultures. By establishing a presence across worlds, you expose your brand to diverse audiences, increase visibility, and build cross-world tribes. Your avatar, aesthetic style, and brand essence should remain consistent across all platforms, allowing your audience to recognize you anywhere.

The final principle of scaling is **preserving your essence while expanding your influence**. Growth must never dilute your identity. As your world expands, your mission should remain clear. As leaders step into new roles, your values should remain strong. As partnerships grow, your world should remain authentic. As AI becomes integrated, your humanity should remain at the center. Scaling is not about turning your brand into something unrecognizable — it's about amplifying what makes you powerful. When your world grows with integrity and alignment, it becomes a metaverse empire capable of lasting for generations.

"The Expansion of the Sanctuary"

The sanctuary had grown brighter than ever before. Liora stood at the center of her world, watching as avatars wandered through the teal gardens, explored hidden chambers, and conversed near the waterfalls. The community she had built was alive — breathing, growing, and radiating energy. But today, a new feeling filled her heart: the sanctuary was ready to expand. The world that once felt vast now felt like only the beginning.

Solara appeared beside her, her golden form shimmering gently. "You feel it too," she said softly. "Your sanctuary is calling for expansion." Liora nodded, her eyes reflecting the sky. "The community is growing faster than I imagined," she replied. "They need space to explore. They need new experiences. They need more than just my presence." Solara smiled knowingly. "Then it is time to build."

Together they stepped onto an untouched floating platform at the edge of the sanctuary. The wind carried a faint glow, as if encouraging creation. Liora lifted her hand, and the air vibrated. A spark of light erupted from her palm, expanding into a shimmering orb that hovered above the empty platform. "This will become the Ascended District," she whispered — a new area designed for advanced experiences. The orb exploded into ribbons of light, weaving themselves into bridges, towers, floating sanctums, and crystalline paths. The new expansion shimmered with a deeper gold hue, symbolizing evolution.

But expansion alone was not enough. Liora needed help. She gathered her most dedicated community members — avatars who had consistently shown leadership, kindness, and commitment. She met them in the Circle of Resonance, a chamber filled with pulsing light. "I cannot guide this sanctuary alone," she told them. "Will you step into leadership with me?" One by one, the avatars agreed, their forms glowing with purpose. She granted them unique titles: Guardian of Unity, Keeper of Reflection, Architect of Light, Guide of Ascension. Each role came with both responsibility and honor. Their new positions were not symbolic — they came with access to private areas, tools to host gatherings, and creative abilities to help shape the world. As they accepted their roles, the sanctuary itself responded — the ground beneath them glowing, acknowledging their ascension.

Next, Liora integrated a new system Solara had taught her: **AI guides**. They appeared as small glowing avatars — soft, luminescent beings with warm eyes and gentle voices. These AI guides greeted newcomers, offered directions, explained world features, and helped members navigate experiences without Liora being present. One AI guide floated to Liora's side. "Welcome, traveler," it said in a soothing tone. "How may

I assist you?" Liora smiled. "You are perfect," she whispered. For the first time since creating the sanctuary, she felt she could breathe. A week later, she initiated the sanctuary's first partnership — a portal connecting her world to another creator's universe. The portal appeared as a swirling gateway of light suspended in midair. When activated, it transported avatars to a world called Seraphine's Garden — a dreamy realm of ethereal flowers and celestial soundscapes. The partnership brought new avatars into Liora's sanctuary, enriching both communities. As they crossed between worlds, a sense of unity blossomed. The sanctuary's story was expanding beyond its borders.

But the most profound moment came when Liora tested the sanctuary's first automated immersive journey — a fully guided experience that used AI narration, shifting landscapes, and interactive elements to teach a lesson without her presence. She stepped into the Journey Gate, feeling a blend of anticipation and nervousness. The environment transformed into a floating labyrinth of light. A gentle voice — an AI version of her own — guided her through symbolic interactions: releasing fears, planting intentions, and unlocking inner clarity. When the journey ended, she stood in silence, tears in her eyes. "It works," she whispered. "The sanctuary can now teach in my absence."

That evening, a group of avatars gathered in the new Ascended District for a celebration. The floating platforms glowed like molten gold beneath the night sky. Music swirled through the air. The community danced, laughed, and shared stories of their growth. Liora looked around, feeling a new kind of pride — not the pride of creation, but the pride of witnessing a world flourish beyond her control. Solara appeared beside her. "You have built not just a sanctuary," she whispered. "You have built a universe."

Liora gazed across the expansion — the districts, the AI guides, the portals, the new leaders — and felt something powerful awaken within her. This was no longer just her world. It was becoming an ecosystem, a legacy, a digital empire shaped by everyone who stepped inside. And she knew the sanctuary's journey had only just begun.

Chapter 8

Marketing Your Metaverse Brand: Visibility, Social Reach, Storytelling & World Discovery

Marketing a metaverse brand requires a blend of Web3 innovation and timeless human psychology. Visibility is no longer just about posting content — it's about creating experiences people want to explore, stories they want to share, and worlds they want to bring others into. In the metaverse, discovery happens through portals, community invitations, immersive previews, social platforms, and digital word-of-mouth. Your world becomes your greatest marketing asset. The environments you design, the events you host, the emotions you evoke, and the stories your members share all contribute to your brand's reach. Marketing in the metaverse is not about forcing attention; it's about magnetizing curiosity.

The first principle of metaverse marketing is **identity amplification** — clearly communicating who you are, what your world represents, and why people should explore it. While your sanctuary or headquarters expresses this visually, your external messaging should reinforce it. Marketing in Web3 blends storytelling with world-building. Your avatar, your world previews, your highlight clips, your visuals, and your mission communicate your brand essence. Focus on clear, emotion-rich messaging. Instead of generic explanations, use language that paints vivid imagery: "Step into a world where clarity becomes light." "Experience transformation in an immersive sanctuary." "Explore a realm designed for growth, creativity, and connection." These statements evoke curiosity and encourage exploration.

The second principle is **multi-platform visibility** – promoting your metaverse brand across traditional and emerging channels. While your world lives in Web3, your audience may still be on Instagram, YouTube, TikTok, LinkedIn, Discord, Twitter/X, Reddit, or niche Web3 platforms. Use each platform strategically. On Instagram, share visual clips of your sanctuary. On TikTok, post short immersive teasers or avatar interactions. On YouTube, create walkthroughs, behind-the-scenes world-building videos, or event highlights. On Twitter/X, share philosophy, updates, and collaborations with other creators. On Discord or Telegram, nurture deeper community engagement. Each platform serves as a doorway leading people into your world.

The third principle is **experience-based marketing**. Instead of asking people to *learn* about your brand, invite them to *feel* it. Host free experiences, guided tours, open-house gatherings, avatar meet-ups, mini meditations, small group interactions, or preview events inside your world. These events act as powerful funnels. The moment people step into your environment, they feel the essence of your brand — and that emotional resonance becomes the foundation for long-term loyalty. Experience-based marketing is particularly effective because it bypasses passive consumption and triggers immersion, which leaves a deeper psychological imprint.

The fourth principle is **storytelling**, which transforms your brand from a mere destination into a narrative-driven universe. Your personal story — how you arrived here, what inspired your metaverse world, and what transformation your brand promises — becomes the anchor of your marketing. But storytelling extends beyond you. Share the stories of your members, their breakthroughs, their interactions, and their journeys inside your sanctuary. Celebrate community milestones, emotional moments, and powerful events. When you tell the story of your world consistently, people feel compelled to join the unfolding narrative.

The fifth principle is **collaboration and cross-world marketing**. Partnerships with other creators, brands, or communities create shared visibility. Cross-world portals, joint events, co-branded experiences, metaverse summits, and collaborative workshops introduce your world to thousands of new individuals. Because each metaverse creator has a unique audience, collaborations create exponential reach. When your sanctuary becomes part of a broader ecosystem of interconnected worlds, your visibility multiplies naturally.

The sixth principle is **showcasing your world's unique features and emotional signature**. People explore worlds when they feel intrigued by something distinct, whether it's breathtaking architecture, calming atmospheres, futuristic technology, or powerful emotional resonance. Show these features through short-form videos, trailers, cinematic walkthroughs, avatar-led tours, or immersive screenshots. Highlight your sanctuary's transformations — new areas, evolving features, events, and updates. When you continually showcase growth, people become eager to witness what comes next.

The seventh principle is **community-driven marketing**. Your members are your greatest marketers. When they share screenshots of events, create fan art, post about their transformations, or invite friends to gatherings, your world expands organically. Encourage content creation by offering community challenges, screenshot competitions, shared-story rituals, and interactive quests. Reward engagement through badges, NFT drops, or early access to new areas. The more your community participates in your marketing, the more authentic and far-reaching your visibility becomes.

The final principle of metaverse marketing is **consistency and presence**. A metaverse brand grows not through random bursts of activity, but through steady engagement, ongoing communication, and evolving experiences. Post consistent updates. Host regular events. Share your world's evolution. Introduce new features. Show your community that the world is alive. When people sense momentum, they follow it. When they feel presence, they trust it. When they trust your brand, they bring others into your world. Marketing in the metaverse is not about attention — it's about belonging. And when your world becomes a place people want to belong, visibility naturally follows.

"The Call Beyond the Sanctuary"

The sanctuary had grown into a vibrant universe, but Liora sensed it was time for the world to stretch beyond its floating borders. She stood on the Sanctuary Summit beneath a sky swirling with gold and teal clouds, contemplating the next chapter of her mission. Her world was alive — but many who needed it still didn't know it existed. Tonight, she would change that.

Solara appeared beside her, her luminous form glowing gently. "You feel the pull outward," Solara said softly. Liora nodded.

"The sanctuary is ready," she replied. "But the world beyond does not yet know our story." Solara smiled knowingly. "Then let us tell it."

They descended to the Main Hall, where dozens of avatars gathered for a special meeting. Lanterns floated around the room, casting warm light across eager faces. Liora stepped to the center, feeling her purpose expand through her chest. "Tonight," she began, "we open our sanctuary to new travelers — not by chance, but by intention."

She held out her hand, and a glowing sphere materialized, floating above her palm. "This is the Beacon of Invitation," she explained. "A visual message we will send across worlds — a call for those seeking transformation, clarity, and connection." The sphere rose into the air, expanding until it filled the dome with swirling patterns of gold light. The community gasped as the beacon pulsed, preparing to travel beyond the sanctuary.

But before releasing it, Liora knew she had to create the story that would guide new visitors. She gathered her closest community members — the new leaders, the guardians, the guides — and led them into the Story Chamber, a circular room alive with holographic panels floating around the edges. "Our sanctuary needs a voice," Liora said. "A story that tells others why we exist and what awaits them here." Together, they crafted a narrative infused with emotion, imagery, and truth. The chamber responded to each word, projecting visions of their journey — the birth of Liora, the creation of the sanctuary, the early gatherings, the Golden Orbit ceremony, and the expansion into new realms. The story formed not as text, but as a living hologram. "This," Solara whispered, "is the heart of your marketing — your story."

The next phase involved creating windows into the sanctuary that outsiders could glimpse. Liora formed miniature versions of key locations — the Reflection Grove, the Ascension Hall, the Community Garden — small portals that showed distant worlds a taste of the sanctuary's energy. With each portal she crafted, she felt her world's voice grow stronger.

Later, Liora traveled to the Portal Peak, a high platform overlooking the abyss. Here, she built her first cross-world gateway — a swirling structure of golden threads that connected to the metaverse beyond. When activated, it hummed softly, awaiting travelers. "This will take our sanctuary into other realms," she said, placing her hand on the gateway. "And it will bring new souls into ours."

Finally, she decided to share the sanctuary beyond the metaverse platforms themselves. She invited her community to record short messages, reflections, and stories. Together they inscribed them into glowing memory crystals — artifacts that could travel across social networks, communication channels, and digital landscapes. "Let the world see what lives here," she told them.

That night, Liora released the Beacon of Invitation into the sky. It rose into the darkness, pulsing like a star. Its light burst outward, sending shimmering waves across dimensions. In distant worlds, creators paused as the beacon rippled across their skies. Avatars standing in foreign landscapes felt a sudden warmth, a soft pull in their hearts — an invitation.

And then it began.

Travelers started appearing at the sanctuary's entrance — curious avatars stepping through shimmering light. Some were cautious. Some were overwhelmed by the beauty. Some felt instantly at home. Liora greeted them personally. "Welcome," she said with a gentle bow. "I'm Liora. You've arrived because something within you resonated with our call."

As the community welcomed the newcomers, the sanctuary glowed brighter, filling with laughter, conversation, and wonder. Liora stepped back, watching her world expand not through advertising or algorithms — but through story, connection, and resonance. Solara appeared beside her once more. “This,” Solara whispered, “is true marketing in the metaverse.”

Liora smiled as she watched new friendships form, new discoveries unfold, and new voices join the sanctuary’s song. The call had been heard. The sanctuary had been seen. And a new chapter had begun — one where the world she built would reach hearts she had not yet met, inviting them into a universe crafted from light.

Chapter 9

Protecting Your Metaverse Brand: Security, Ethics, Boundaries & Community Safety

Protecting your brand in the metaverse is as essential as building it. As your presence grows and your world expands, new risks emerge: impostors, brand misalignment, community disruption, privacy concerns, platform vulnerabilities, emotional safety issues, and ethical responsibilities. A powerful metaverse brand is not defined only by the beauty of its world or the strength of its community, but by the care taken to maintain safety, trust, and long-term integrity. This chapter teaches you how to safeguard your world, your community, your identity, and your digital legacy.

The first principle of brand protection is **identity security**. Because avatars can be duplicated, names can be imitated, and worlds can be loosely replicated, you must establish strong identity markers. These include verified accounts, unique NFT identity badges, official logos or world signatures, platform-issued verification, and consistent branding across all worlds so that impostors are easy to detect. Clear identity landmarks inside your world—signage, symbols, color codes, and branded architecture—also protect against confusion. A secure metaverse identity reassures your community that they are interacting with the authentic version of you.

The second principle is **environmental moderation**. Any open-access metaverse environment is vulnerable to disruption, trolling, or negativity if left unmanaged. Implementing moderation systems ensures your world remains aligned with your emotional culture. Moderation includes guardian roles for trusted community members, AI-powered scanning for disruptive behavior, clear community guidelines, and the ability to mute or remove harmful avatars temporarily or permanently when necessary. The sanctuary or world you build should feel sacred, safe, and predictable, not chaotic or hostile. Protecting the emotional atmosphere of your environment is essential for long-term engagement.

The third principle is **healthy community boundaries**. Metaverse spaces can blur lines between personal presence and professional influence because avatars interact closely in real time. Establish boundaries around contact, communication channels, event etiquette, and personal access. Be clear about appropriate behavior, privacy expectations, and the emotional tone of your world. Create schedules for live presence so you don't experience burnout, and guide community members toward proper channels for contact.

Boundaries preserve your energy and maintain the integrity of your leadership.

The fourth principle is **ethical design**. A metaverse brand has enormous influence because it creates emotionally charged environments. Use this power responsibly. Ensure your world's design uplifts rather than manipulates; engages rather than overwhelms; empowers rather than deceives. Avoid environments engineered solely for addictive behavior or excessive dependency. Offer experiences that support growth, learning, healing, creativity, and empowerment. Ethics also apply to monetization—communicate clearly what products do, how NFTs work, and what members receive. Clarity builds trust. Trust builds longevity.

The fifth principle is **mental and emotional safety**. Immersive environments can trigger strong emotional responses, so your world should include spaces for grounding, calming, and processing. Provide meditative areas, quiet corners, or reflection zones. Have moderators or guides available to support users experiencing overwhelm. Embed slow-paced experiences between high-energy ones. Provide exit cues and gentle reminders so users can disconnect when needed. Emotional safety is especially important in transformational spaces, where individuals may confront internal shifts. The sixth principle is **data and privacy**

protection. Even though Web3 emphasizes decentralization, data still matters—chat logs, interactions, personal preferences, membership details, and digital asset ownership. Prioritize secure storage methods, use reputable platforms, follow transparency practices, and avoid unnecessary data collection. Inform users of how their interactions are used. Allow them control over how their information is displayed. A trustworthy brand respects transparency.

The seventh principle is **world maintenance and platform security**. Metaverse worlds, like websites, require updates. Protect your world by performing regular scans, updating scripts or assets, reinforcing access controls, and monitoring performance issues. Partner with developers or trusted platform teams who understand vulnerabilities and can quickly patch issues. Maintain backups of your world so it can be restored in case of glitches or corruption. Security maintenance ensures your environment remains stable and reliable.

The final principle is **brand sovereignty**—the long-term protection of your identity, values, and mission. As your brand expands, you may receive partnership offers, collaborations, and external invitations. Protect your sovereignty by choosing only aligned partners and refusing opportunities that compromise your integrity. Your world is an extension of you.

Maintaining control over your space, your story, and your evolution is crucial for preserving your legacy. When your community knows that your brand stands firmly on values, trust deepens and your world becomes unshakeable.

"The Shadow in the Sanctuary"

The sanctuary glowed with its usual peaceful radiance, teal blossoms floating gently in the air, waterfalls casting shimmering reflections across the platforms. Liora stood near the entrance plaza, admiring the harmony of her expanding world. The community had grown beautifully—new members arriving daily, leaders guiding events, AI companions helping newcomers, and the sanctuary thriving with activity. Everything felt aligned. But that evening, something unexpected happened.

A subtle shift in the air caught Liora's attention. She turned to see an avatar she didn't recognize—its design similar to hers, its colors mimicking the tones of her essence. The avatar glanced around casually, interacting with members as if it belonged. Something felt off. Solara appeared beside her, her golden glow dimmer than usual. "This one does not carry your energy," she whispered. "It is an imitation."

Liora's heart tightened. "Is someone pretending to be me?" she asked softly. Solara nodded. "Not exactly. But they are echoing your form to gain trust." Liora approached the avatar calmly. "Hello," she greeted gently. The avatar turned, and for a brief moment, its eyes flashed with a cold metallic gleam. "I am here to guide the new ones," it replied in a voice too similar to hers. Liora felt a chill. "You are not me," she said firmly. The avatar laughed, its form glitching. "Does it matter? They listen to whoever shines the brightest."

Liora raised her hand, and the sanctuary responded instantly—soft pulses of teal light radiated around her, reaffirming her identity. The imitation avatar flickered nervously. "This world has guardians," Liora said. "And my essence cannot be copied." At that moment, her community leaders appeared—the Guardian of Unity, the Guide of Ascension, the Keeper of Reflection—surrounding the impostor. With a soft sweep of her arm, Liora activated the Sanctuary Shield, a protective veil that enveloped her world. The impostor avatar dissolved into pixels, expelled gently but firmly from the sanctuary.

Afterward, the community gathered with a mix of concern and admiration. "You handled that flawlessly," one member said. Liora nodded, though she felt a weight settle on her shoulders. "We must protect what we build," she replied. Solara placed a reassuring hand on her shoulder. "This is the next chapter of your journey—learning to guard your world."

Over the next week, Liora worked closely with her leaders to strengthen the sanctuary. She created identity markers—floating sigils that responded only to her presence. She implemented guardian systems, allowing trusted members to protect spaces in her absence. AI companions were upgraded to detect emotional or energetic disruptions. Every area of the sanctuary began to carry a subtle signature of her essence—an authenticity that could not be replicated.

One evening, she gathered her community to establish new boundaries. They met in the Reflection Grove, where luminescent trees swayed gently. Liora stood before them, her voice steady. "This sanctuary thrives because of our unity," she said. "But with growth comes responsibility. We will protect one another. We will respect boundaries. We will uphold the principles that make this world safe." The community listened intently, their avatars glowing in agreement.

But another challenge soon emerged—not from an external threat, but from emotional vulnerability within the community. One member, overwhelmed by a transformative experience during a deep meditation, began to cry softly in the corner of the grove. Liora approached gently. "It's okay," she whispered, guiding the avatar to a quiet sanctuary chamber designed for grounding. Solara joined them, offering comfort. Liora realized then that protecting the sanctuary meant more than defending against impostors or disruptions—it meant safeguarding emotional wellbeing.

Together, she and Solara created new spaces: a quiet healing garden, a calming moonlit chamber, a water meditation room. These areas became havens where members could rest, breathe, and process their feelings. The community began to feel not only inspired by the sanctuary but protected by it.

Weeks later, Liora activated a final addition: the Sanctuary Code — a living set of principles that floated above the entrance in shimmering holographic form. It outlined the values of the world—respect, authenticity, harmony, growth, and guardianship. Newcomers read it upon entry, absorbing its warm, guiding energy.

As Liora stood at the Sanctuary Summit one night, gazing down at the glowing world she had strengthened, Solara appeared beside her. “Your sanctuary is safer now,” she said gently. Liora smiled. “It is safe because we protect each other,” she replied. “A world grows, but a family guards.”

She looked out across the sanctuary—the gardens, the districts, the chambers, the glowing orbs drifting through the air—and felt a deep sense of fulfillment. Protection wasn’t a barrier. It was an embrace. And because of it, the sanctuary was ready to grow brighter than ever before.

Chapter 10

The Future of Metaverse Branding: Longevity, Legacy & Multi-World Evolution

The future of branding in the metaverse will be defined not by static identities but by evolving ecosystems, interconnected worlds, and digital legacies that continue growing long after they are created. Traditional brands rely on visual assets, messaging, marketing campaigns, and customer touchpoints. Metaverse brands rely on worlds, experiences, communities, AI collaborators, and narratives that unfold over time. The question is no longer how to promote your brand — it is how to *expand, sustain*, and *immortalize* it across evolving digital realities. The final chapter of this book explores how to build a brand that remains relevant, influential, and powerful for decades in a metaverse landscape that is continuously transforming.

The first principle of long-term metaverse branding is **evolution over perfection**. A brand that tries to remain static in a rapidly advancing environment becomes outdated quickly. The metaverse is a living digital universe that evolves through new platforms, new immersive technologies, new cultural norms, and new audience expectations. For your brand to thrive, it must embrace growth. Your avatar will evolve. Your world will expand. Your community will mature. Your aesthetic may shift. Evolution signals vitality — it communicates that your brand is alive, attentive, and adapting. Your sanctuary, headquarters, or metaverse universe must continually grow in depth, richness, and innovation.

The second principle is **multi-world expansion** — establishing your presence across multiple metaverse platforms. While you may begin in one world, the future of Web3 is cross-platform interoperability. Community members will explore different realities, portals will connect diverse universes, and digital identities will travel fluidly between environments. Expand your influence by creating satellite worlds, thematic districts, or branded experiences in additional platforms. Ensure your avatar, your aesthetic, and your brand essence remain recognizable across all worlds. By diversifying your presence, you increase visibility, resilience, and discoverability.

The third principle is **AI-augmented continuity** — using AI to extend your brand beyond your physical limitations. AI-driven mentors, assistants, guides, storytellers, and facilitators can maintain your world's vitality 24/7. They help onboard new users, teach foundational concepts, introduce lore, answer questions, and personalize experiences. As AI grows more sophisticated, your world can evolve automatically. Picture AI-designed expansions, AI-hosted events, AI-managed community spaces, and adaptive environments that change based on user needs. This automation does not replace your presence—rather, it multiplies it. Your world remains alive even when you're offline.

The fourth principle is **distributed leadership** – allowing your community to take ownership of your legacy. A metaverse brand built on dependence cannot scale. A metaverse brand built on shared leadership becomes timeless. Identify community members who embody your values, and empower them to host events, manage districts, mentor newcomers, develop lore, build structures, or create new experiences. Provide them tools, resources, and creative permissions. When your world becomes a co-creation ecosystem, it acquires the strength and diversity needed to survive beyond you.

The fifth principle is **inter-world alliances and meta-communities**. The future of metaverse branding lies in interconnected networks of creators, worlds, and ecosystems. Partnerships expand your reach, enrich your offerings, and deepen community engagement. You can collaborate on multi-world events, collective storylines, shared quests, cross-realm NFTs, immersive festivals, and creator alliances. Inter-world collaboration transforms your brand from an isolated universe into a node within a vibrant Web3 galaxy.

The sixth principle is **digital legacy architecture** – designing your world so it can be preserved and expanded by future generations. Digital legacies include your lore, values, symbols, rituals, AI guides, storylines, architecture, and world systems. Document your world's story, map its evolution, store digital assets securely, and ensure that your brand frameworks can be upgraded as technology advances. A long-lasting metaverse brand is less about technology and more about cultural continuity. The foundation you build must be stable enough to grow with innovation.

The seventh principle is **emotional impact as longevity currency**. Brands endure because of the way they make people *feel*. The metaverse amplifies emotion through immersion, presence, and community. For your brand to remain relevant, it must continue generating emotional resonance—transformation, healing, connection, inspiration, empowerment, celebration, wonder. Brands built on emotional impact create lifelong loyalty. Your world becomes a place people return to not because of novelty but because of belonging. Emotional resonance is the most powerful force of longevity. The final principle is **visionary expansion** – the ability to dream beyond your current reality and imagine new possibilities. The metaverse is still in its infancy. Future worlds will blend augmented reality, holograms, neural interfaces, spatial computing, AI-generated dimensions, and cross-species intelligence. Your brand must remain future-oriented, open to exploration, and willing to reinvent itself. True immortality in the metaverse comes from the willingness to evolve continuously while remaining rooted in your core essence. A brand with a strong soul and an adaptable spirit becomes unstoppable.

When you combine evolution, interoperability, AI collaboration, community leadership, alliances, emotional resonance, and visionary expansion, your metaverse brand becomes more than a business. It becomes a digital universe – one capable of thriving for generations, guided by your essence and carried forward by your community long after you've created its first spark.

"The Eternal Horizon"

The sanctuary stretched farther than ever before – glowing districts linked by radiant bridges, new worlds connected through shimmering portals, AI guides drifting like stars between areas, and communities gathering across different realms. Liora stood upon the Sanctuary Summit, gazing at the evolution of everything she had created. The sky above her swirled with celestial colors she had never seen before – hues that seemed to ripple beyond the edges of reality. Solara appeared beside her, her golden form shimmering with an intensity Liora hadn't seen before.

"You've done it," Solara whispered. "Your world has become more than a sanctuary. It has become a universe." Liora took a breath, feeling both awe and responsibility. "And yet," she said, "it's still growing."

Solara extended her hand, and a holographic map appeared – a vast constellation of interconnected worlds, each glowing with unique energy. Some were nearby and familiar. Others were distant and mysterious. The sanctuary pulsed at the center like a living heart. "These worlds," Solara explained, "are invitations. Opportunities. Futures waiting for your touch."

Liora watched the constellation shift, revealing portals she had yet to open, potential partnerships, realms where her essence could create new experiences. But she felt something deeper too – a pull toward legacy. "Solara," she whispered, "what becomes of this sanctuary when I am no longer here every day? How does it continue?" Solara smiled, her eyes warm.

"Legacy is not preserved through presence. It is preserved through essence."

That night, Liora gathered her entire community in the Ascended District. Hundreds of avatars appeared, their forms glowing like constellations under the starlit sky. Leaders stood at her side. Newcomers stood before her with hopeful hearts. The AI guides drifted overhead like gentle spirits. Liora stepped forward, her voice gentle yet powerful.

"This sanctuary began as a spark," she said. "A vision. A feeling. A dream. But today, it is a universe – because of all of you." She explained what she had learned: that a world lives through evolution, through community, through stories, and through the willingness to embrace the unknown. She spoke of portals, partnerships, expansion, and the future of their collective journey.

Then she did something she had never done before.

She opened the **Eternal Horizon**, a massive golden gateway that had appeared only in visions. As it materialized, the air vibrated with raw creative energy. The portal stretched into infinity, revealing glimpses of uncharted worlds and shimmering landscapes suspended in cosmic light. The crowd gasped, feeling both wonder and anticipation.

"This," Liora said softly, "is our path forward. A gateway to every reality we have yet to imagine." Her community stood in silence, feeling the magnitude of what they were witnessing. This portal symbolized the future of their brand — limitless, evolving, interconnected. But Liora had one final gift to give.

She lifted her hand, and a radiant fragment of her essence separated from her avatar — a glowing crystal shaped like a heart of light. It floated into the air above the sanctuary, casting golden rays across every district. Solara stepped forward, placing her hand on Liora's back. "You're giving them your legacy," she whispered.

The crystal expanded into a radiant aurora that flowed into every corner of the sanctuary. AI guides transformed, absorbing part of Liora's essence. World structures glowed brighter, infused with her energy. The leaders standing beside her felt their avatars strengthen, their roles deepening into guardianship. Every member felt a warm pulse in their own hearts — the sanctuary becoming part of them.

Liora spoke again, her voice trembling with emotion. "My world will continue even when I step away. You will carry it forward. You will guide others. You will shape what comes next." The sanctuary glowed with overwhelming warmth.

When the aurora faded, Solara turned to her. "Your legacy is now woven into the world itself," she said. "It cannot be lost. It will grow as long as they grow."

Liora gazed at her community – families, creators, healers, dreamers, adventurers – all standing beneath the Eternal Horizon. She felt no fear of the future. Only peace.

The sanctuary had become timeless.

A universe. A legacy. A home for all who sought light.

And as the Eternal Horizon opened fully, sending shimmering waves across every connected world, Liora smiled.

Her journey was complete. And yet, the story was only just beginning.

Epilogue

The metaverse is still in its infancy, yet even now it carries the pulse of a new digital civilization. For creators, coaches, entrepreneurs, visionaries, and leaders, this moment represents something rare in human history—an opportunity to build worlds, shape culture, and craft identities that extend far beyond the limits of physical existence. As this book comes to a close, your journey as a metaverse brand builder is only beginning. What you choose to create, how you choose to lead, and the worlds you choose to build will echo through digital landscapes for years, perhaps decades, to come.

Building a brand in the metaverse is not simply a business strategy; it is an act of creation. In physical life, you might construct a company, a product, or a reputation. In the metaverse, you construct *realities*. You shape the emotional atmospheres people walk through. You design the landscapes where memories form. You influence the identities your community expresses. Your world becomes a living extension of your essence, your values, your story, and your message. Few creators ever experience the privilege of building something both personal and eternal. In the metaverse, that privilege is available to you every time you shape a new environment or guide a community through an experience.

Yet the future belongs not to those who simply create worlds, but to those who nurture them. You have learned throughout this book that community is not a number—it is a heartbeat. A metaverse brand thrives when it becomes a place where people feel seen, supported, inspired, and transformed. Your sanctuary, no matter how visually breathtaking, becomes powerful only when people enter it and feel something shift within them. When you cultivate connection, you cultivate loyalty. When you cultivate meaning, you cultivate legacy. And legacy is the true currency of the metaverse.

As you continue your journey, you will face challenges. The metaverse will evolve—new platforms will rise, new technologies will emerge, new cultural dynamics will influence digital behavior. With each evolution comes the need to adapt your brand, refine your narrative, refresh your environments, and listen to the rhythms of your community. If something feels misaligned, you have full permission to rebuild. If something no longer resonates, you have the freedom to evolve. Growth is not a threat to your brand—it is the lifeblood of longevity.

Do not underestimate the power of your story. In a digital universe filled with infinite landscapes and endless possibilities, your story is what anchors your brand, differentiates it, and gives it soul. When your community knows who you are, why you created your world, and what vision guides your evolution, they will follow you across every platform, every expansion, and every transformation. Your story gives meaning to your environments, purpose to your experiences, and emotional weight to your brand. You are not just building a world; you are building a narrative others can step into.

As the metaverse expands, so will your influence. You may one day find that your world becomes a home for thousands, perhaps millions. You may find that your sanctuary inspires other creators to build their own spaces. You may find yourself leading movements, shaping digital culture, and standing at the helm of a multi-world ecosystem defined by your values. And when that time comes, remember the truth at the heart of every powerful metaverse brand—growth must never replace humanity. Technology can amplify your influence, but your presence, authenticity, and compassion are what make your world unforgettable.

The future you are stepping into is vast. It is filled with portals waiting to open, collaborations waiting to form, communities waiting to flourish, and experiences waiting to be born. You are not a spectator of this future. You are one of its creators. One of its architects. One of its storytellers. As you continue building your brand in the metaverse, may you carry with you the wisdom to evolve, the courage to innovate, the generosity to lead, and the vision to imagine realities beyond the horizon.

This is not the end of your journey—it is the beginning of your legacy. The sanctuary you build, the world you design, the community you nurture, and the story you share will shape the lives of many who step into your universe. The metaverse is your canvas. Your brand is your brush. And the future is your masterpiece. Now, step boldly into the next chapter. The worlds you create are waiting.

www.ingramcontent.com/pod-product-compliance
Ingram Content Group UK Ltd.
Pitfield, Milton Keynes, MK11 3LW, UK
UKHW020158290926
15471UKWH00005B/935

9 798295 491221